7 Timeless Principles *of* INVESTING

AuthorHouse™
1663 Liberty Drive
Bloomington, IN 47403
www.authorhouse.com
Phone: 1-800-839-8640

Published by AuthorHouse   06/01/2012

ISBN: 978-1-4772-1264-6 (sc)
ISBN: 978-1-4772-1265-3 (e)

Library of Congress Control Number: 2012909989

"Investing is not easy. There are a lot of facts and figures out there, and the excess of information can be disorienting even for market professionals. The beauty of Barry's book is that he offers a series of basic principles that apply to the most experienced trader as well as the investing novice. Rules that should be heeded in bull and bear markets alike. Most importantly, he stresses that investors find the right portfolio mix to suit their needs and temperaments. In the end, investing is a very personal endeavor, so you can't get better advice than that."

—Gregg Greenberg, financial journalist,
TheStreet.com, CNBC's "Closing Bell"

"This is an ideal book for seasoned investors and all others who aspire to understanding our financial markets. Simple and concise, Barry James' seven principles are easy to grasp and so eminently sensible you can be forgiven for wondering why all financial advisers don't heed them. The answer, of course, is that Barry's prescription takes enormous discipline to implement. As a James client for years, I have been well rewarded by the team's wisdom and control. And I sleep well at night!"

—Polk Laffoon IV, journalist, former vice president
for Knight Ridder corporate relations

7 Timeless
Principles
of
INVESTING

By Barry R. James
President/CEO, James Investment Research, Inc.

authorHOUSE®

James
Investment
Research, Inc.

P. O. Box 8, Alpha, Ohio 45301
p 937.426.7640 | *f* 937.426.7097
JIR-INC.COM

DISCLAIMER

This book is designed solely to provide helpful information and encouragement to our readers based on our opinions, ideas and experiences. It is not a recommendation to purchase or sell the securities of any of the companies or investments discussed herein. The author and publisher are not offering it as legal advice, accounting guidance, or any other financial or professional service. Every investor is different, and federal and state laws vary, thus the advice and strategies contained herein may not be suitable for your situation. Before beginning any financial program, the reader should consult a competent professional for assistance.

References are provided for informational purposes only and do not constitute endorsement of any businesses, websites or other sources. Readers should be aware that the websites listed in this book may change.

While best efforts have been used in preparing this book, the author and publisher make no warranties or guarantees of any kind and assume no liabilities of any kind with respect to the content of this volume.

Neither the author nor the publisher shall be held liable or responsible to any person or entity with respect to any liability, loss, damages or risk, professional or otherwise, incurred or alleged to have been incurred as a consequence, directly or indirectly, of the use or application of any of the contents of this book.

This book is dedicated to
my dad,
my family,
our clients,
and my coworkers.

Acknowledgments

The principles described in this book were developed in the 1960s and 1970s by Dr. Frank James, who I want to recognize and thank. He has been a wonderful father as well as a terrific mentor.

Special appreciation is due to Dr. Fall Ainina, CFA, and Ria Megnin for their assistance in editing and finishing this book.

I give my deepest gratitude to my wife Joyanna for her support and encouragement. I've never accomplished anything of lasting value without her by my side. I'm also indebted to my children, Matt, Alycia and Alex. Their creativity and passion have been inspiring.

I'm also grateful for my mother, Iris James; my brothers, Frank James III and David James; and each of my coworkers. You lived through all of this, seeing if it would work, seeing it come to fruition. Neither our company nor this book would have come to be without your support.

Contents

Foreword

For anyone generally interested in investing, and particularly for those who want to manage their portfolio themselves, this book is a very valuable, even essential, read. At long last, we get to look into the investment principles that have guided a very successful investment management organization for many years. I have so often wondered what made Frank James and his sons Barry and David so successful at managing investment assets. I believed it must be a set of complex formulas easily within the grasp of Frank, educated as an engineer, but certainly not within the reach of people of common sense ("mere mortals") like ourselves. This book has put that fear to rest.

7 Timeless Principles of Investing describes sound principles—many of which are so very basic, they are often overlooked—in an easy-to-understand style which can often be penetrating. For that, we need to thank Barry. He clearly has worked hard to share his best in this book, and you will feel his passion for the principles and the business of investing. So, thanks, Barry.

The lessons he outlines are indeed timeless. For instance, you will often see the word "discipline" in this book. Barry understands how emotional investors can become. We have a strong tendency to become panicky and sell near market lows, and to become euphoric and buy near highs. Even professional investors can get caught up in the day-to-day, week-to-week swings which invariably tempt them to abandon their discipline. What a mistake! Read Barry's story of the investor who, in 1999, decided that investing in the hot new Internet company was the answer. This is not as unusual a story as one might think.

Stay disciplined, the book urges. Nothing could be more important to successful investing.

The second and perhaps most valuable insight in this book is the careful integration of time and good timing in successful investing. I have always believed, as Barry confirms, that time, not merely timing, is the secret to success as an investor. The biggest success stories I have heard as a professional investor are about stock investments that appreciated over years, not days or months. Yet I have also seen the importance of timing. As the book explains in detail, it's important to be good at timing, not great. *7 Timeless Principles of Investing* expertly explains using relative strength to refine timing techniques. This is highly valuable investing knowledge, and Barry explains it well.

Third, the book highlights the importance of diversification, in case you make some timing mistakes along the way. As Barry points out so insightfully, having 17 or more stocks in a portfolio might sound like diversification, but if they are all technology stocks, the portfolio is anything but diversified. Putting all one's eggs into one basket makes little sense in most aspects of life, and it's particularly so in the business of investing.

Fourth, Barry understands the importance of having discipline when you need to sell an investment. As he states, "when you sell is more important than what you buy." As many of us have learned over the years, quite a few investors are good buyers. Not nearly as many are good sellers. And yet, as Barry outlines so clearly, this is one of the simple principles essential to investment success.

Of the many important lessons contained in this book, the one I value most is that of relative performance. I have always suspected that the biggest mistake an investor can make is to ignore the performance of the financial markets. Barry is quite right that, in the world of investing, "a body in motion tends to remain in motion." Stocks which have tended to outperform the market over long periods of time tend to continue to outperform. Stocks that underperform are most likely underperforming for a reason, even though you may not know it. As an associate of mine often says, "Stick around. You'll find out the reason." The story of Bear Stearns should not be missed. Barry's appreciation for this fundamental concept in investing is deep, as well it should be. Again, Barry's guidance is simple, insightful, right.

If people want to manage their own investment assets, they should read this book first. Those of us who have been investing for years and learned many of these lessons the hard way know how easy it is to understand the principles, but how many of us can follow them? James Investment Research can and has, and as a result, has been very successful. Now I understand the reasons for their success.

Thanks again, Barry James, for sharing your approach with us, for making it so clear and, as a result, useful.

Hugh Johnson, chairman and CIO
Hugh Johnson Advisors
February 29, 2012

7 Timeless Principles *of* INVESTING

Preface

When my daughter, Alycia, was in high school, she asked me to give a presentation on investing to her school. I said yes, of course—but I was worried. How could I share 30 years of book learning and real-world experience in just 43 minutes?

Just a few days before the big presentation, I realized what I needed to communicate. Instead of trying to impart dozens of specific techniques for making money, I could pass along the timeless principles followed at my family's company, James Investment Research, Inc. (JIR), principles that have helped our clients avoid millions of dollars in losses while making millions more in profits over the years.

If you're reading this book, chances are you're thinking about the future. Maybe you're a new parent, looking for ways to save for your child's education. Maybe you've just received an inheritance, and you're wondering what investment approach will make the most of the windfall. Maybe you're facing retirement and hunting for tips on growing your money to meet your lifestyle.

Will a safe, steady, conservative approach work best for you? Or bold and constant aggression, targeting the most likely market winners?

This book is designed to help you better understand your options no matter what your financial goals or where you fall on the investing spectrum. I'll be sharing the tips and guidelines I've used in hundreds of presentations with classrooms and clients alike. You'll also get the chance to go deeper and explore how the principles described here apply to you, through guide sheets and questionnaires designed to help you get started on a successful financial path.

The JIR motto is: "Investing For A Lifetime." With our long-term focus and steady pace, we're a lot like the tortoise in the old fable. We don't always make headlines, and we're far less entertaining to watch than the dashing hare. But just like the tortoise, while the market pitches, leaps and dives, we have a record of steadily progressing toward success.

Our team's results have drawn interest from *The Wall Street Journal* and expert financial media including *Barron's, Bloomberg, Smart Money, Kiplinger's, CNBC, Bloomberg TV* and *Fox News Business*. Our daily radio show and weekly research reports are followed by thousands. We don't claim to know everything or be right in all cases, but after four decades in business, our approach continues to perform well.

How do we protect our clients' assets so they can grow in periods of both prosperity and economic gloom? It's simple: our record shows that we tend to avoid mistakes that cost investors money and (even worse) time.

The roots of our approach go back to 1972, when my father, Col. Frank James Jr., was head of the graduate logistics school of management at the U.S. Air Force Institute of Technology. One of his department's accounting instructors was also a certified public accountant, whose clients wanted their retirement funds managed.

The instructor had been following my father's research on the markets, as well as how he managed the James family's money, and encouraged him to share his insights as a professional adviser. At his encouragement, JIR was formed.

In 1973, my father hired me as the first paid employee of our firm. My job as a high school student was to call our broker each day the market was open and chart stock price movements. Although I went on to an eight-year career as an instructor and fighter pilot with the U.S. Air Force, I returned to JIR in 1986 as a research associate.

Our family's company grew and grew. Our commitment to minimizing risk without limiting returns led to consistently strong results for our clients. We attracted a team of professionals, including PhDs and CFAs. Our investment committee members have been with us an average of over 20 years.

Today, our team draws on our decades of research as we manage investments worth more than $3.0 billion. Our time-tested approach helps us to avoid many of the false steps that cost so many investors millions, and to recover faster and more thoroughly after market dives.

This book is another opportunity to share our philosophies with you. Besides learning about our 7 Timeless Principles, you can access our latest insights, tips and resources at jir-inc.com or by talking with us directly. You can reach JIR's exceptional team at 1.888.426.7640. We have the skills and knowledge to help clients like you navigate the ocean of investing advice, rumors and emotions—and meet your life goals.

Welcome to the JIR investment family,

Barry R. James, CFA, CIC
President/CEO of James Investment Research, Inc.

Introduction:
Investing Isn't Gambling

*"Don't gamble. Take all your savings and buy some good stock
and hold it 'til it goes up, then sell it.
If it don't go up, don't buy it."*

—Will Rogers

To set the stage for understanding the *7 Timeless Principles of Investing*, I'd like to make sure you and all new investors know what investing is not.

Some people view the stock market as a casino. Others think of gambling as a form of investing. Neither is true, so let's dispel the myths by highlighting the three major differences between investing and gambling.

Key difference No. 1: **The odds favor investors**

When I gave a talk about investing to the eighth grade classroom, I asked if anyone wanted to play against me in a game of blackjack. I gave one young lady $100 and said "If you win, you can keep the $100. My house rules of blackjack apply, and as the dealer, I win all ties." I then dealt the cards. I had a queen showing, worth 10 points, but she showed the class a really nice hand. She had a jack showing and a 10 in the hole—20 of the 21 points needed to win.

The suspense built, and the students were excited. If I ended with 19 points or less—or overshot and scored 22 or more—she would win the $100.

Then I turned over my second card, and the class let out a sigh of disappointment. It was a king, worth 10 points. House rules said I won any tie, so I got my money back.

As you may have guessed, I'd set up the cards that way to make my point. (You'll note I didn't take her money, just got my own back—not every investment adviser is crooked). My daughter's classmates learned that the odds favor the house and that games of chance are often rigged.

The gaming industry knows how to use those odds to take advantage of gamblers. In blackjack, even if you play perfectly, the house still has a 0.5 percent advantage. I explained to the class how much this helps a gaming company. In 2010, for instance, MGM Resorts took advantage of such odds to produce revenues over $6 billion.

In the financial industry, however, the "house" is, essentially, investors, and we stand a much higher chance of success. That's because the odds are even more in our favor. While short-term returns in the stock market vary considerably, it's hard to find long-term periods when shareholders lost money. For instance, one broad measure of the stock market, the S&P 500, rose by an average 10.2 percent a year between 1935 and 2010.

This leads me to the second difference between investing and gambling: time.

Key difference No. 2: **Time favors investors**

Gamblers usually look for immediate results. They aren't concerned with what happens in the long run. But investors deposit time along with their money. The longer the period of time, the more likely a solid investment is to succeed.

When I meet with clients, I tell them to avoid the stock market if they want to use the money before at least three years have passed. Anything less would, essentially, be gambling—or as those in my industry euphemistically say, "speculation."

The final key difference between gambling and investing deals with how your money is used while it's at risk.

Key difference No. 3: **Investors have a higher purpose**

In gambling, there is great risk, but the money doesn't serve any cause but the gambler's gratification.

Investing is designed to bring long-term benefits to society as a whole. When people put money into companies and communities, new factories and warehouses are constructed, staffs are hired, services are expanded and infrastructure built. As a public company grows, shareholders have a say in what's happening, helping to shape policy and practices while holding business leaders accountable. All of these can have a positive effect on many people, rather than only enriching a small group.

Now that you understand the key differences between gambling and investing, you understand the foundation the 7 Principles were built on:

- *Smart investments favor the investor.*

- *Only long-term investing makes sense.*

- *Real investing benefits the broader community.*

Let's build on this understanding as we explore ways to make the most of your money in the future.

The First Principle:
Know Yourself

"This above all: To thine own self be true."

—*William Shakespeare*, Hamlet

"What does knowing myself have to do with investing?" In a word, everything. At James Investment Research, Inc., we've learned that truly successful investors achieve their goals based on their temperament, even if it means they don't make the highest possible returns. They match their investments to their comfort levels so they can stay with their choices for the long run, putting the odds of success in their favor.

So how do you get to know yourself as an investor? Start by asking yourself this question:

"If I owned a stock, and the price dropped 10 percent, what would I want to do?"
>   **A) Sell immediately**
>   **B) Sell once the stock gets back to its original price**
>   **C) Buy more**

It's good to know your gut reaction to a loss, because it tells you a lot about yourself and what types and styles of investments you would favor. It also tells you where your weaknesses lie, and what types and styles of investments you should avoid.

Let's look at the possible answers one by one.

A) Sell immediately. You may have a temperament that's averse to risk and losing capital. This doesn't mean you can't outperform the market as an investor! Finding the right mix of conservative investments and smart risks is the key to both comfort and success for you, and a good investment adviser can help you find both.

B) Sell once the stock gets back to its original price. You may be what I call an "evener." You're not comfortable with risk and may not have a long-term strategy for investing. This approach could undermine the long-term performance of your investments.

You might be better off keeping money in the bank. Better yet, team up with a good adviser to learn more about the markets and find a strategy for success that works for you.

C) Buy more. You may have a high level of risk tolerance and would not be afraid of suffering a loss in your investments. You'll likely be bold in your investment decisions, perhaps even rash. Even if you don't always take an in-depth approach to making a decision, you have confidence in your decisions. Coupled with the ability to see things differently than the crowd, your contrarian approach can be very, very useful in investing.

There is, in fact, a fourth option for savvy investors when their stock price drops 10 percent. And that is:

D) Follow the guidelines you made in advance for this situation. When you understand the basic principles of investing and apply discipline, you'll find success regardless of temperament. Success doesn't necessarily mean getting rich quickly, but it does mean meeting your goals for financial sustainability over time.

This concept of discipline is an often overlooked key to investing. Once you know yourself and have found an approach that fits your temperament, you need to stay with it. The problem many investors have is jumping from one style to another style and losing sight of their goals along the way.

In the late 1990s, during the bull market of the dot-com boom, JIR's returns looked paltry when compared with more aggressive, technology-only styles. Even as clients left us to pursue hot new options with seemingly infinite returns, we kept our discipline. We wouldn't buy the latest Internet stock with no earnings and even fewer prospects of future earnings, because we know this is one of the worst long-term methods of buying stocks.

Although the crowd went wild over these kinds of stocks, we were ultimately proven right. Sticking with our discipline kept us from losing large sums of money on these shaky investments, and after the mania, many of our former clients returned with renewed trust.

We have learned that we can make people rich, but it takes time, and they have to stay with us. The same is true in the mutual fund industry. Studies have shown that most investors have lower returns than the mutual funds they invest in, because they buy when funds have run way up, then sell after prices fall. As a result of following their emotions instead of showing discipline, these investors end up with worse results than if they stayed in a fund for the long term.

The best approach to building wealth through investments, then, is to understand yourself and what fits your investment temperament. Then, develop the discipline to override your emotions and see your commitment through to a successful end.

The Second Principle:
Avoid Losing Money

"Never lose money."

—Warren Buffett

Warren Buffett, one of the world's wealthiest people, has two oft-quoted rules for investing. The first is the opening quote of this chapter, "Never lose money." The second is: "Never forget rule number one."

For starters, this means avoiding all scams.

The FBI and Securities & Exchange Commission investigate thousands of financial fraud claims each year, uncovering Ponzi and pyramid schemes like Bernie Madoff's, advance-fee schemes that do no more than collect "initial fees and advance tax payments" from their victims, and high-yield investment fraud that promises plenty of returns in stocks, property, jewels, businesses . . . for "little to no risk."

So how do you avoid becoming another victim of a scam? Our philosophy is: if it sounds too good to be true, it probably is.

Here are some steps you can take to confirm whether an investment is legitimate or a fraud.

- **Confirm the claims.** If returns are said to be "guaranteed," take a hard look at what backs those returns. Many scams claim that governments, banks, institutions or hard assets have insured the deal, and offer pictures and reams of paper to prove it. Tell the salesperson you plan to independently check with the group (using contact information you find through sources besides the person you're speaking with), as well as the Better Business Bureau, your State Securities Office and the federal Securities and Exchange Commission. Ask what might turn up. You'll scare the typical scam artist away.

- **Get direct access.** Often, asking to visit a site and meet additional people who actually do the work can clear away any smokescreens. Many scams depend on keeping information and access tightly restricted.

- **Remember your discipline.** Even with legitimate investments, it's still important to be careful. If everyone seems to be making tons of money, remember: when everyone has discovered a good deal, it's usually long gone. This advice will keep greed at bay and money in your pocket.

As my father says, "Common sense is the best defense."

Besides not falling for scams, following our "avoid losing money" principle also means not risking more than an investment is worth. Preserving capital doesn't mean your money is never at risk—investments always carry a measure of risk. But you should be rewarded appropriately for the risks you take.

For instance, one of JIR's clients fell victim to risking more than an investment was worth. In 1999, our client had reached his 60s and was looking forward to retirement. We had been managing his Individual Retirement Account (IRA, a tax-deferred savings account) for over 15 years. But in the heady days of the dot-com boom, this individual said the $500,000 in his account wasn't enough for him to retire the way he wanted. He saw the potential for great returns by investing in one of the hot new Internet companies.

We advised against the move, since the company had no earnings and no real prospects for earnings. Nevertheless, he insisted on buying the stock. We then recommended he only take a small portion of his money to put in this stock. Unfortunately, he did not follow our advice.

The stock came out around $16, and then almost immediately doubled to $32. But the ensuing weeks were unkind. The stock price faltered. Our client took the rest of his money and bought additional shares.

Less than a year later, the stock was trading for pennies, and our client's retirement money was essentially gone.

How can you avoid making a similar mistake? Follow the principle of knowing yourself, and then stay disciplined so you don't lose money.

One more reason to avoid unnecessary risk is that you're not just risking the initial price of the investment. You're risking the time it will take to make up for the loss.

Here's an example from my presentation to the junior high classroom. They had a pool of $14,000 they were to invest over the year, tracking its performance in the stock market. I pointed out that if they had to pay for just a 10 percent loss, they would have to work at a job paying better than minimum wage, with no taxes withheld, for eight-hour shifts every day for a month! That's a lot of time.

Remember when you're tempted to put your money into an overly risky investment: Your time is valuable, and making up losses isn't the best use of it.

The Third Principle:
It's Not What You Own—It's When

"Timing isn't everything. It's the only thing."

—Barry R. James, with apologies to Vince Lombardi

The goal of winning drove every decision legendary coach Vince Lombardi made for his team. But for investors, the goal is good timing.

When I speak to college finance classes, I ask students to tell me the most important word in investing. Sometimes I hear "diversification," or "correlation," but my ears perk up when someone mentions the word "time."

That's when I explain that, bottom line, what you own doesn't matter as much as when you own it. JIR's approach to investing is based on this concept, and every decision we make comes back to the timing of the investment.

Let me give an example. JIR has reviewed price performance for the Dow Jones Industrial Average for a period in excess of 50 years. If an investor had missed the best 10 days in the Dow, he or she would have missed about half the total return for those 50 years. But if that same investor had missed the 10 worst days, his or her performance would have more than doubled.

This isn't to say anyone can manage their investments to perfectly hit or miss specific days, but it does show the importance of when their money is in the mix.

Another example involves focusing on when you own a specific stock. If you owned Netflix in 2010, for instance, you had the best performing stock in the S&P 500, with a $100,000 investment turning into $318,640. But in the first nine months of 2011, Netflix fell 35.5 percent, wiping out $113,117 of that gain. Here, timing was key for JIR. At the beginning of 2010, our clients owned more than 100,000 shares of Netflix. At the end of the year, we owned less than 3,000 shares. We had sold out completely by the end of the first quarter in 2011, dodging major losses.

You may notice that JIR didn't sell at the exact high. Even though everyone wants to buy before prices rise dramatically, then sell right at the very peak, no one has been able to invent a process to successfully do this. But that kind of perfection isn't our goal, anyway. Why? Perfect timing is not required to make excellent profits. Just good timing. Our aim is to recognize and act on important signals in the market that don't require the precision of capturing an exact low or high.

Let's look at the components of good timing. The "when" concept applies to:

- *when to buy,*

- *how long to hold,* and

- *when to sell an investment.*

When to buy

When it comes to the actual stock and when to buy it, we take a long-term approach. We want to own shares in a company that will be around for many years to come and will likely hold up better than most other stocks when the market falls. No one knows the exact timing for a major advance in a stock's price, so we also want to own shares we would be comfortable holding for a reasonable length of time. And, we want to buy shares in a company with a good probability of advancing strongly in the next six to 12 months. Our research, going back to the 1920s, shows stocks that are already rising at a pace better than the market (called relative strength) are likely to continue doing so. If we can find that type of stock while it's experiencing a temporary pull-back, we think we have a pretty good entry point. However, this doesn't preclude us from buying stocks reaching new heights.

Having determined an optimal minimum holding period, we eliminate stocks that don't meet our standards. This narrows the field considerably, and often runs counter to conventional Wall Street wisdom. We think Wall Street puts too much emphasis on what to buy and not enough on when to sell. One of our research reports shows that Wall Street analysts average about eight "buy" recommendations for each "sell" recommendation. Our firm runs almost exactly the opposite. In other words, we are first concerned with what stocks we shouldn't own in the next six to 12 months.

How long to hold

When you do choose a stock to invest in, you'll want to have a plan for how long you'll hold it.

For example, let's say you could choose whether to hold shares of communications technology giant Qualcomm in 1999 or in 2000.

In this exaggerated example, if you chose 1999, you would gain more than 22,000 percent. If you chose 2000, you would lose more than 60 percent.

What's important to note is that the company remained the same and produced excellent profits both years. The changes in price were purely the product of market volatility.

This example shows how critical it is to decide ahead of time whether you will take a strict buy-and-hold approach—making an investment and leaving it there for a predetermined amount of time, regardless of performance—or one based on changes in the value of the stock, company or earnings. Your approach will depend on your temperament—would you be willing to tolerate such major downturns as that seen with Qualcomm? Or would you want to sell the stock once its value, growth or loss hits a certain amount?

When to sell an investment

The most important decision in investment timing is when to sell. This component is so important that according to our studies, if we followed our predetermined sell timing for stocks chosen completely at random, the resulting theoretical portfolio would actually outperform the stock market (S&P 500).

Let me be clear: JIR doesn't select stocks randomly. But the tests confirm what we have long suspected: when you sell is more important than what you buy.

We base our criteria for when to sell on what we identify as the factors most likely to affect a stock's price in the next six to 12 months. We have tested hundreds of factors, and they essentially fall into three categories: valuation, earnings and past price performance. Using our predetermined time frame, we score each stock based on its relative attractiveness compared with the other 8,500 or so stocks we follow. This is not the only way to determine when to sell, but we want a discipline that aligns with who we are as investors and—just as important—is repeatable.

I've explained a time frame to consider and some factors to use when looking at stocks. Each of us needs to do the same no matter what the investment is. Start with the end in mind: when will you sell? After you have this discipline in place, you can better determine a minimum holding period, then examine when and what you will buy. This process will leave you better prepared and lessen your anxiety.

The bottom line is: it doesn't matter what you own if you don't own it at the right time.

The Fourth Principle:
Hang On to Winners, Sell Losers

"Hang on to winners, sell losers.
If it ain't broke, don't fix it."

—Bert Lance

How do you know which stock to sell? First, keep in mind that your remaining stocks should be the ones with the best potential for advancing. Second, check with your financial or tax adviser about any tax consequences your sell decision could have.

After that, your choice is simple but not necessarily easy: whether to sell your biggest losers. Why "not easy?" Almost all of us have a strong aversion to taking a loss. We secretly hope that if we hold on for just a little longer, our investment will rebound.

I tackled this concept while talking with the eighth graders by asking if any had gardens at home. Many did, and had spent plenty of hours working in them.

I asked, "When your parents sent you out there, did you go out with the instructions to pull up all the tomato plants and carrots, then throw them away? Did they ask you to water and fertilize the weeds?"

The students laughed. And yet, I told them, plenty of people take that exact approach with their portfolios. In the vain hope of keeping their portfolio "even," they will hang on to a stock that goes down in value relative to the market, while rapidly selling any stock that rises to capture profits.

The problem with this approach is that stock movements usually follow Newton's Law of Inertia: a body in motion tends to remain in motion. My father identified a connection between this law and the stock market in 1967, when he discovered a key investing rule now known as relative strength. In his doctoral dissertation, he studied every stock on the New York Stock Exchange from 1926 to 1960. He found that the stocks which outperformed the market over long periods of time continued outperforming into the future. This was the first empirical proof that the "random walk" theory, which says stock performance is completely unpredictable, is not totally correct.

In other words, if a stock isn't doing very well, there's usually a reason, and it's not likely to do well in the future. But it's a fair bet that stocks whose companies have done well in the past and haven't changed their practices will, despite brief downturns, continue on that path of success.

For instance, in 2009, Wal-Mart stock lagged behind the rest of the market. But just a year before, it was one of only two Dow stocks that rose in spite of the financial crisis. Sure enough, in 2010 and 2011, Wal-Mart shares rebounded and, in fact, reached new yearly highs.

Bear Stearns, on the other hand, began underperforming the stock market early in 2007. Since its earnings weren't doing well, either, we sold our shares in the middle of the year. In a little over a year,

Bear Stearns had dropped from \$172 a share to \$2, and was sold to JP Morgan Chase.

Here's one of the most extreme examples of this principle—hanging on to winners and selling losers—in action. In 1992, shares of the technology company Dell rose 180 percent. But a year later, its price fell by 52 percent—enough to frighten almost any investor away. Those who stayed, however, were rewarded when the stock grew at an unbelievable rate in the next six years—climbing more than 14,000 percent!

The strongest argument for dropping stocks with a poor record but holding on to successful stocks when they dip in price is a simple mathematical principle: you can lose only what you put into the market, but your potential gains are unlimited. In other words, while stocks can only fall 100 percent, they can rise 1,000, 2,000, 3,000 percent and beyond.

So to refresh and rejuvenate your basket of stocks, you need to periodically prune the selections, just as you would prune a garden. As with a garden, your pruning shouldn't cut down blooming flowers so that weeds can prosper.

Invest in stocks that are growing over time, and you're far more likely to land on the right side of the market.

The Fifth Principle:
Avoid Following the Crowd

"When everyone's discovered 'a good deal,' it's long since gone."

—Barry R. James

(With apologies to every astute investor who already knows this.)

There's a concept in investing called a mania, and it's got a lot in common with its psychological roots. It's what happens when a large number of investors' emotions cloud good, solid reason. Remember the person mentioned in Chapter 3, who lost a fortune by following the crowd into the dot-com mania?

Manias aren't necessarily easy to see until the dust clears. But there are some warning signs.

- Manias are characterized by a rapid and extreme run up in prices that are not justified by fundamental values.

- It becomes "common knowledge" that this investment is a "sure thing."

- A pathway for the average person to invest opens up. Yet, everyone still believes they can get out in time if prices start to drop.

- Finally, anyone who gives a warning is deemed old-fashioned and irrelevant. We know, because it happened to us at the end of 1999. In that year, the Internet stock index rose in excess of 160 percent. It appeared as though money was lying around on the street just waiting to be picked up. One client told me that he thought 40 percent a year returns would continue into the future. We had seen similar speculative episodes in 1972-73 and 1987 in the general stock market. More recently, we saw it in 2005-6 in real estate. In both cases, the markets soon tumbled significantly. However, in all of these cases, the crowd was shouting "buy, buy, buy."

So how can you tell if the crowd is right? Here's what we look at to see if a market is too popular for safe investing:

- Follow the smart money. Track what those with smart and not-so-smart reputations are doing.

- Examine the corporate actions of the "hot" stocks. Are they buying or selling their own shares in the open market? They tend to be smart.

- How about the people who work in the companies—are they buying or selling their shares? They are often right.

- Read surveys of investor sentiment. As a rule, when the crowd "discovers" a good deal—it's usually too late to get in on it. But if you're in, the moment the price starts to reverse, that may be a strong signal to consider pulling out. (JIR uses multiple measures to identify when it's time to sell.)

- Check the levels of cash in mutual funds. Having a lot of cash indicates the crowd has less confidence in the market. This can be a good time to buy.

- Watch the price of investments that folks use to hedge their investments. The lower they go, the less worry the crowd has and the more worry you should have.

- Track financial headlines. Generally, the more optimistic they are, the less you want to own the investment they tout.

- Whether it's Internet stocks, real estate or gold, when everybody and their brother tout it, you can be assured you aren't the one who will benefit. Even if you do, it likely won't last long.

Besides not chasing the same investments as everyone else, a good way to get ahead is to look for quality investments the crowd ignores. Bonds, for instance, are rarely the most popular place for people to put their money. But over the course of the rocky 2000s, they showed some of the best possible returns.

The Sixth Principle:
Diversify, Diversify, Diversify

"Don't put all your eggs in one basket."

—Old English proverb

No matter how carefully you choose an investment, disaster can strike. Sometimes it is literally, as in the case of major hurricanes, droughts or earthquakes. Sometimes it is political in nature. Markets can be rocked by coups, government incentives or austere laws and regulations. When you diversify, you reduce your exposure to such risks.

Take the case of Enron. If you worked for them in the 1990s, had your retirement money in company stock, and only bought natural gas and electric-related securities, you would have been in real trouble.

Likewise, if you'd put all your money in Internet stocks with the hope of retiring in 2001, you'd likely still be working today.

If you invested solely in real estate between 2005 and 2008, you're not likely to see that money back any time soon.

Most savvy investment advisers will encourage you to diversify: invest in different sectors of the economy, and don't keep all your money in one asset class—you should have some stocks, bonds, some real estate and some hard assets as well. If calamity strikes one area, it won't wipe you out.

Diversification should trickle right down to which stocks you own. Have a variety. Statistically speaking, proper diversification requires having more than 17 stocks in your portfolio. If you're just starting out as an investor, you can have less than 17 as you work up to full diversification. But if that's more work than you want, you should probably invest in something that's naturally diversified, like most mutual funds.

However, you can own many stocks and still not be diversified. We've had clients come to us with all of their equity holdings in the energy industry, or in technology stocks. Make sure you choose companies that do different things. For example, Wal-Mart is different from Exxon, but it's not much different from Target.

Diversification doesn't just involve what you invest in. It also depends on when. If you put all your money into the market today, and the market falls 10 percent the next day, you've lost 10 percent of your wealth. If, however, you put half your money in today, and save the rest for another time, you'll have cut your loss in half, five percent.

Not only does diversifying the timing of your investments help mitigate losses, it makes it easier to get started. If the market fell, you could take solace in knowing you didn't have all your money in the market. If, however, the market kept going up, you could take solace in knowing you had some money in the market. The idea is that you stay in the game without having everything on the line.

That's the way JIR approaches money management. We don't usually try to make all the decisions or investments for our clients on a single day. We will take months or even longer to find the best opportunities for investing a portfolio across the markets. This helps us protect our clients' funds while improving their chances of financial success.

The Seventh Principle:
Let Time Work for You

"Time is money."

—*Benjamin Franklin,* **Advice To A Young Tradesman**

The final principle sums up all the rest.

Having made smart, diversified investments that fit your temperament, it's time to sit back and let your decisions play out over time.

If someone buys a house today, then tries to sell it tomorrow, they incur a great deal of transaction costs going both ways. Now that the real estate bubble is over, they probably wouldn't see enough increase in the property's value to cover those costs. In fact, the next day, the home's price may actually be down. If they wait a few months or years, however, their chances of seeing a profit from the investment go way up.

The same is true when we look at stocks. High turnover (day trading) is unlikely to produce big gains, and any gains made would be reduced by the transaction fees involved. This is consistent with the overall role of the stock market, since investors are buying ownership in companies intended to produce over a long period. As companies grow, other people will want to buy in, causing the price to rise over months and years. Anything shorter term would be speculation—and smart investing is not about gambling.

That doesn't mean it isn't tempting to chase the latest hot stocks and Initial Public Offerings. We all hear stories of meteoric rises that boost the rare, lucky investor's fortunes. And on average, the stock market does produce strong annual returns.

But not every year! In 1931, Wall Street had a one-year loss of 43 percent. More recently, the stock market (S&P 500) saw annual downturns of 22 percent and 37 percent in 2002 and 2008, respectively.

The way to beat the odds of landing in a bear market is to broaden your time frame. That's why it's so important to work with advisers or money managers who actually manage money, following a particular strategy that honors a core philosophy, rather than chasing the latest data on last year's winners or the hot new stocks making the media rounds.

It's the reason dollar-cost averaging has become a popular investing approach. To minimize the risk of bad timing in owning a stock, investors commit to putting the same amount of money into a particular stock at regular intervals. If the stock price goes up from one investment period to the next, fewer shares are purchased. If the stock price goes down, the money will buy more shares. Over time, the average price paid per share will often be lower than if all the shares had been purchased at once.

It's also good to remember that historically, while bonds, money market instruments and other conservative options are less subject to fluctuations, stocks historically outperform them over long periods of time.

All investments are affected by large-scale factors such as interest rates, inflation and supply and demand. Just remember—while any of these can have a significant short-term impact on returns, over enough time, investments tend to perform as expected for their category.

How to Apply the Seven Principles

Practice what you know and it will help
to make clear what now you do not know.

—**Rembrandt Van Rijn**

Hopefully, you now understand the Seven Principles: Know yourself; Avoid losing money; It's not what you own—it's when; Hang on to winners, sell losers; Avoid the crowd; Diversify, diversify, diversify; and Let time work for you.

Step 1: Conduct a self inventory, such as Guide 2 in the back of this book, to determine your general needs and goals as an investor and your comfort—or discomfort!—with risk.

Step 2: Outline what you want to accomplish with the money you are investing. In setting out these goals, you'll identify the time periods involved and your target returns.

Step 3: Create a set of guidelines that rule your investments. This is where you start building the discipline that fits your temperament. (Guide 3)

Step 4: Identify techniques you'll use to measure your investments' performance, and how often you'll use them to make sure you're on track. For example, you can use popular stock indexes listed online or the published rate of inflation.

Step 5: Determine your investing style. What's the best fit for your temperament? Knowing this allows you to select an investment structure you can comfortably stay with for the long haul. This final step is the most involved, but the most essential to your financial success.

At the back of this book, we provide a self-inventory that can help identify your investment style, along with a general structure for balancing risk and returns for each style.

If you feel overwhelmed, or don't have the time or desire to figure out what to invest in, you can hand over the responsibility to someone else. But it's still crucial to know your temperament. You'll need to find a money manager or investment adviser who matches your comfort level and can support your goals. All too often in our business, we hear of investors who didn't find a good match, became uncomfortable with their money managers and jumped ship at just the wrong moment. For tips on what to look for in these professionals and how to make sure they line up with your temperament, read the bonus guides that follow this closing chapter.

At JIR, we've followed the same guiding discipline—*7 Timeless Principles*—for 40 years. We're confident in our approach, because we've found them to be applicable to almost any investment. But they are just the foundation when it comes to investing. Managing your wealth and securing your future are lifelong processes, and there's always more to learn and explore. And so our final advice is to keep growing. Stay in touch with your financial advisers. Track what's happening with your funds and become familiar with websites and magazines that promote financial literacy. Spend time at your local library or with organizations that host financial education workshops—for example, the American Association of Individual Investors. Stay curious.

Remember, investing isn't only for highly qualified experts. You have the instincts, wisdom and, now, the *7 Timeless Principles* needed to see your assets grow.

Best wishes in your investing future.

In Conclusion

I knew a CEO who joked with his employees. "We have a retirement plan so your wife's next husband won't have to work as hard as you did." What a funny way of saying, "You can't take it with you when you go." I like how my old friend Doug Roe rephrased it. "You can't take it with you, but you can send it ahead."

I think he's right. Our deeds of generosity and kindness go beyond this life. We may leave behind our earthly possessions, but that's all the more reason to wisely handle the opportunities we've been given. We will have an impact on generations to come.

As I close, I ask you to consider one last investing principle. It concerns what I think it is the greatest investment opportunity of all-eternity. This principle starts with a question: What would it take to convince you the creator of the universe wants to be your friend? You may or may not believe in God or eternity. That's your business. It's not my job to convince you otherwise. Still, I hold a deep conviction that God believes in you, has a great plan for your life and wants you as a friend.

I think you were made exactly the way you are because God wanted someone just like you. In all of human history, there has never been, nor will there ever be, another like you. I sincerely believe you were made to show some aspect of God's goodness that no one else could. If you are intrigued and would like to test this final principle, please fill in the blank: "God, if you are real, show it to me by _____."

I have faith you will be surprised by the response.

To learn more about the God-honoring principles that have helped shape my life and JIR's business, visit my personal website at barryrjames.com.

      —Barry

Bonus Guides

GUIDE 1

First Steps to Start Investing

The hardest part of investing is taking the first step. Most people don't know where or how to begin, and so they delay starting for years.

They may always have trusted parents or spouses to handle financial issues for them. They may be intimidated by the paperwork and legalities. Or the self-imposed pressure to invest perfectly from the get-go—feeling like their entire financial future is at risk—is too intense. Meanwhile, their money is earning 0.15 percent when it might be able to earn 15 percent.

The key is to simply get started and not try to jump from kindergarten to college in one go. First, find a professional investment adviser or firm to work with, one with a strong history of success, and an approach that matches your investing style. The following bonus guides will help with both these tasks.

Then, have your adviser help you open an account with a small amount of money, either from savings or reallocated from existing accounts. As you get more comfortable with investing, you can add to it. Have money automatically transferred from your paycheck to your new account. Develop the discipline of paying yourself first each month and learn as you go.

Your first discussion

When you first seek to hire a financial adviser, he or she will most likely ask you to bring in all your statements—checking, savings, debts and bills—and spend some time talking about your situation. If they don't listen to you, don't hire them.

Some common questions you'll be asked: How much income do you have? What are your resources? Do you have any debts? What are your expenses? Are you dealing with any life circumstances or long-term commitments that could affect your financial goals?

You'll also talk about your objectives for investing. How much money will you need to achieve the lifestyle you want? How much market risk are you comfortable with?

Only after completing the assessment should your adviser start exploring options for where you invest your money.

The learning never stops

Once you've begun the investing journey, you can start the lifelong process of perfecting how your money grows.

- Read articles, books and websites on investing. (See Suggestions for Further Reading in the back of this book for some ideas)

- Take adult education classes on personal finance and investing and basic investment courses.

- Sign up for an online workshop.

- Talk with investment-savvy friends.

- Join an educational organization like the American Association of Individual Investors.

- Learn the terminology of investing: equities, markets, benchmarks, commodities, high-yield, etc. (See Guide 5)

- Study investment performance and how to measure it. How does what happens with markets affect your accounts? How can you hold on to money in down markets?

- As you grow more confident, get technical. Learn how to get the most out of your investments through tax breaks, account types, adjustments in fee schedules, individual stocks, and more.

GUIDE 2

What Style Investor Are You?

Self-evaluation Worksheet & Analysis

Answer each question honestly, then add up the total points.

1. What percent of your assets that are set aside for investments are you considering placing in these funds?

   ___ 75-100% **(2 points)**

   ___ 50-74% **(4 points)**

   ___ 25-49% **(6 points)**

   ___ Less than 25% **(8 points)**

2. Please choose the most accurate description of your primary investment goal for this portfolio.

   ___ High Current Income: To maximize the generation of investment income (interest and dividends) while avoiding the risk of downturns in the value of your account. **(1 point)**

   ___ Income and Growth: To achieve a balanced return of current income and modest growth of principal. **(2 points)**

___ Long-Term Growth of Principal: To emphasize long-term growth of principal, while avoiding excessive risk. Short-term volatility will be tolerated when consistent with the volatility of a comparable market index. (**3 points**)

___ Aggressive Growth of Principal: To maximize total return with volatility equal to or greater than that of the stock market in the short-term and over the investment horizon. (**4 points**)

3. What type of investment strategies are you most comfortable using?

___ Aggressive investment styles using whatever it takes to get return, including selling stocks short, using future contracts, options, etc. (**4 points**)

___ I am comfortable investing in stocks. (**3 points**)

___ I prefer investing in mutual funds rather than individual companies, because I don't feel comfortable following individual stocks. (**2 points**)

___ I prefer to avoid stocks because they are too risky. (**1 point**)

4. What time horizon do you deem appropriate in evaluating the performance of your portfolio? In other words, how long would you hold the account before seriously considering making a change?

___ One to three years (**1 point**)

___ Three to five years (**2 points**)

___ Five years or more (**3 points**)

___ A complete market cycle (possibly 10 to 15 years) (**4 points**)

5. Given this time frame, what do you consider a fair return?

___ 6 to 8 percent **(1 point)**

___ 8 to 10 percent **(2 points)**

___ 10 to 12 percent **(3 points)**

___ Higher than 12 percent **(4 points)**

6. An increase in investment "total return" is usually associated with an increase in the acceptable level of fluctuation, or volatility, in the portfolio value. Please indicate below the single item that best describes investment risk for you:

___ Not achieving goals set in advance **(4 points)**

___ Making less than the rate of inflation **(3 points)**

___ Significant fluctuation in portfolio value—a large loss in total portfolio **(2 points)**

___ The chance of a large loss in a single security in the portfolio, regardless of the overall portfolio performance **(1 point)**

7. Select the hypothetical portfolio with the five-year investment performance that best reflects your preference for your portfolio. *Numbers show investment performance in order for Year 1 through Year 5, with the final number listing the 5-Year Average Return.*

    ___ +5% +7% +6% +4% +5% +5.6% **(2 points)**

    ___ +4% +12% +9% -1% +11% +7.0% **(4 points)**

    ___ -3% +27% +21% -6% +16% +11% **(6 points)**

    ___ -14% +34% +40% -8% +30% +16.4% **(8 points)**

8. When do you plan to make your first withdrawals?

    ___ 4 to 6 years **(1 point)**

    ___ 7 to 10 years **(2 points)**

    ___ 11 to 16 years **(3 points)**

    ___ More than 16 years **(4 points)**

9. The amount and frequency of cash withdrawals from funds affects how your portfolio should be structured. Which of the following situations do you consider most applicable to your funds?

    ___ No substantial withdrawals in the next 10 years **(4 points)**

    ___ No substantial withdrawals in the next 5 years **(3 points)**

    ___ Withdrawals will be less than contributions for the next 5 years **(2 points)**

    ___ Withdrawals could exceed contributions for the next 5 years **(1 point)**

10. Approximately what portion of your total investment assets are in your employee/employer retirement savings program?

___ Less than 25 percent **(1 point)**

___ Between 25 and 50 percent **(2 points)**

___ Between 51 and 75 percent **(3 points)**

___ More than 75 percent **(4 points)**

11. When risk is high, so is return—and when return is high, so is risk. What is your comfort level regarding investment risk, the possibility of losing part or all of your investment dollars?

___ I would only select investments with very low risk/return. **(1 point)**

___ I am willing to accept small amounts of risk and principal fluctuations for better returns. **(2 points)**

___ If it improves the chance of increasing my returns, I am willing to take on additional risk with part of my investment account. **(3 points)**

___ I want to achieve maximum long-term returns, and I am willing to assume a high degree of risk to do it. **(6 points)**

___ I am willing to invest all of my investment account in an investment that has the potential to pay a big return, regardless of the risk. **(8 points)**

12. If you owned a stock and it fell 25 percent, what would your gut reaction be?

___ Sell it immediately **(1 point)**

___ Buy more **(2 points)**

___ Wait until the price returns to the level I bought it, then sell it. **(3 points)**

___ Do nothing **(4 points)**

RESULTS

Your total score may reveal your investment philosophy and what percentage of your assets you'd feel comfortable investing in equities (stocks, securities and other ownership interests), rather than bonds and cash.

20 or less	**31-40**	**51+**
Very Conservative	Moderate	Very Aggressive
0% equity	50-80% equity	70-100% equity
21-30	**41-50**	
Conservative	Aggressive	
30-70% equity	60-90% equity	

GUIDE 3

Four Steps to Investment Discipline

No navigator can set a ship on its course, then go to sleep, and expect that ship to arrive safely at its original destination. The same is true in finances. The best investment plan in the world will fail if you and your adviser don't track its performance in the context of the market.

Here are four key steps that can help you stay on course:

1. Determine your investment style.

Use self-assessments and work with your adviser to identify how much risk you're comfortable with and what types of investments match your style. (See Guide 2)

2. Determine your goals.

Identify your financial goals and time frame, estimate the money you'll need to meet those goals, and factor in any taxes, expenses and liabilities that may be involved.

3. Set your criteria for measuring performance.

How will you know if your investments are on track? What are your triggers for action? Set parameters for risk, identify performance benchmarks, and set time periods for when you'll measure potential or existing investments against those benchmarks.

4. Implement discipline.

- Review any potential investment thoroughly.
- If it meets your predetermined purchase criteria, buy it.
- Until it meets your predetermined sale criteria, hold it.

Potential sale criteria:

- Price drop of a preset percentage
- Ratios/charts turning poor
- Major change in economic environment
- Expiration of time horizon for holding it

Sale criteria to avoid:

- Modest changes in analyst ratings
- Media hype
- Rumors
- Chat room recommendations

GUIDE 4

How to Choose a Money Manager

You've searched for financial managers online. You've read magazines and compared recommendations from national groups. You've talked with your family, friends, and colleagues. You've narrowed the list of financial advisers to those with the right balance of solid performance and personal attention. Now, how can you tell if your soon-to-be partner in protecting your bright financial future is trustworthy?

Simple—find out how they rate on "the 4 P's"—Philosophy, Process, Personnel, and Performance.

Philosophy. This forms the basis of all investment decisions.

- What is their philosophy of investing?

- Does it match yours? Just like a marriage, if it doesn't fit, it will fail.

- Can you stay with this philosophy a minimum of five years?

- Does it make sense? Is it logical? Or is it complex and hard to follow?

Process. If the decision-making and implementation process for putting the philosophy into action isn't well thought out, the firm may have problems.

- Does the process fit the company's philosophy?

- Does it make sense, or is it too complex to follow?

- Can it be implemented on a repeated basis, producing consistent results?

People. Who are the personnel? What experience, background, success and ethics do they bring to the table?

- Are they capable of doing the job and implementing the process?

- Do they inspire confidence and trust? If not, the relationship will never last.

- Do they have a passion for the work?

- Do they invest in their own funds?

- What kind of stability exists in the work force? How does the company keep its top people?

- What is the likelihood the company will stay in business in its current form?

- Are there any legal or ethical issues with the people or firm?

Performance. How has the company followed its philosophy and process over time? Do these managers demonstrate consistency in their decisions, or do they change with the latest trends of the market?

- Are the numbers reasonable? How are the numbers constructed? Are they from just one account, or a whole group of accounts?

- Are the numbers audited, and do they conform with GIPS (Global Investment Performance Standards) and SEC (Securities & Exchange Commission) standards?

- Can you verify the money manager's claims of performance using public records, including the records of the funds they manage?

- Make decisions on more than raw numbers. Remember: you can sell performance, but you cannot buy it.

- Be sure to get explanations of better-or worse-than-expected returns.

- If performance was better than the philosophy called for in a certain period, watch out. This may mean the company was not following its own approach—or worse, they may be cooking the books.

- If you want to buy low and sell high, you first have to buy low. Sometimes the best time to start with a manager is when their style has been out of favor for a period of time.

Managing Your Money Manager

Meanwhile, you'll need to "manage your money manager." Once you've found a solid investing team, chosen a portfolio that fits your style, set the benchmarks and agreed on strategies most likely to help you meet your goals, you need to stay involved.

Don't take a hands-off approach to your portfolio. And don't let your money management team off the hook with an annual statement comparing returns to market indexes or other money managers.

The bottom line is you are responsible for your investments.

- Communicate your financial goals, risk comfort level, and preferred strategy to your money managers. Make sure you're on the same page before committing to any investment changes.

- At least once a quarter, check your investments' performance. If concerned, talk with your managers and compare their decisions with the investing strategy you have in place.

- Make sure your philosophy is being maintained and your investments are producing the results you planned for, even if it means changing managers.

A word of caution. Some investors check performance so often, they drive themselves to distraction because of the volatility of the market. Remember: The point of having a solid investment philosophy and strategy is to let you and your investment team manage your money, not let your money manage you.

GUIDE 5

Glossary of Investment Terms

When you talk with financial advisers, they may use a lot of unfamiliar terms. Ask them to slow down and explain what they mean. A good adviser will appreciate the chance to connect, educate and make sure he or she is on the same page with a client.

Still, it's important to have a working knowledge of basic financial language. Here are some of the most common words and concepts you'll hear as you start to work with money managers.

GENERAL TERMS

Asset allocation
How different types of investments are organized in a portfolio in order to minimize risk and maximize returns, according to the investor's long-term goals.

Benchmarks
A specific set of investments, typically a market index, that a particular investment is compared against to measure its performance.

Capital gains and losses
The difference between what was initially paid for an asset and what it was sold for. If the difference is positive, it's a capital gain; if otherwise, it's a capital loss.

Dividend
The portion of a company's profit paid out to shareholders instead of being reinvested in the business. The company's board of directors decides how much, if any, will be distributed.

Dollar-cost averaging

A technique for minimizing the risk of investing at the wrong time by regularly investing the same amount of money into a particular stock. If the stock price goes up from one investment period to the next, fewer shares are purchased. If the stock price goes down, more shares are purchased. Over time, the average price paid per share is often lower than it would have been if all of the shares were purchased at an inopportune time.

Earnings

The net profit a business shows over a certain time period. Investors often use this information along with market context and other factors to determine whether the company's shares are worth what they're currently selling for.

Equity

Broadly, the value of an investment after all debts are paid off. Often refers to stocks or other securities where the holder owns a portion of the company or investment.

Financial market

A venue for buying and selling assets such as stocks, bonds, commodities and currencies based on the items' current value and market demand.

Gains & losses
(realized and unrealized)

When the value of an item is different from its original cost or market value, it's considered an unrealized gain or loss until the item is sold, at which point the difference becomes realized.

Indexes

A market index is a set of similar investments whose performance, compared with its value at a particular starting date, demonstrates the performance of an entire market and can be used as a measuring standard for individual investments.

Interest

The amount of money paid to a lender or investor in compensation for their risk and lost opportunities for other investments. Factors affecting interest rates include the size and risk of the loan or investment, the length of time it's held, inflation, market value and more.

Portfolio

A collection of simultaneously held investments. Hopefully it is designed to protect the initial principal by minimizing risk, while maximizing its growth through potentially lucrative holdings.

Securities
A contract that can be bought or sold representing a financial asset, including stocks and bonds.

Shares
A portion of a company's value that's sold to raise capital and can be traded in financial markets.

TYPES OF INVESTMENTS

401(k)
A retirement plan where employees contribute a portion of their pay to a tax-deferred investment account, usually a mutual fund, and employers often make matching contributions.

Bond
A bond is a loan you make to a government or corporate entity, usually from one to 30 years, that earns interest based on how likely the loan is to be repaid.

Treasury
A bond issued to the federal government. Considered one of the most secure investments.

Agency
A bond for a government-sponsored entity. Somewhat less safe than treasuries; usually safer than corporate bonds.

Corporate Bond
A bond for a profit-making business. These range from extremely risky to extremely secure.

High Yield Bond
A bond with a higher than average risk of default and commensurately higher interest or dividends for investors.

Municipal/Tax Free Bond
Bonds issued to government entities ranging from airports to school districts to actual municipalities. Interest earned on such bonds is usually exempt from federal, state and local taxes.

CD
Money held by a bank, credit union or similar institution for a fixed amount of time, generally six months to five years, in exchange for a higher interest rate than a traditional savings account.

Commodity
In the financial sense, commodities are products with a value determined by the market as a whole rather than by individual characteristics, i.e. coal, electricity, oats, gold, foreign currencies, etc. They are usually bought and sold on exchanges that set standard amounts and levels of quality.

International investment
A non-U.S. stock or bond. Often included as a portion of investment portfolios as a diversification strategy.

IRA
A retirement plan for individuals, who invest either tax-deductible funds and pay taxes on the eventual value (traditional IRA), or taxable funds that are tax-free upon withdrawal (Roth IRA).

Mutual fund
A collection of stocks, bonds, cash and other securities managed by a team to meet specific investment goals for a pool of investors.

Real estate
A piece of land, its natural resources (such as water, plants and minerals), and any buildings on it. Real estate can be residential, commercial or industrial.

Stock
Investors in a corporation pay for shares, or stock, that represents a percentage of the company's assets and earnings. In return, they anticipate growth of principal or dividends. Common stocks may grant the holder voting rights at shareholder meetings; preferred stocks give the holder the right to receive reimbursements before common stock holders if the company is liquidated.

Market Capitalization
A measure of a corporation's value, calculated by multiplying the number of its common shares by the price of an individual share.

Large cap
Corporations with a market capitalization of $10 billion or more.

Mid cap
Corporations with a market capitalization between $2 billion and $10 billion.

Small cap
Generally, a corporation with a market capitalization between $300 million and $2 billion.

Suggestions for Further Reading

James Investment Research, Inc. recommends the following books for continuing your investing education:

How to Make Money in Stocks—A Winning System in Good Times Or Bad by William O'Neil

The Little Book That Beats the Market by Joel Greenblatt

The Neatest Little Guide to Stock Market Investing by Jason Kelly

The Intelligent Investor by Ben Graham

A good list of books for investment beginners from *The Wall Street Journal* can be found at *http://wsjbooks.com.*

E-books on investments are available from the American Association of Individual Investors at *http://www.aaii.com.*

About the Author

Barry R. James, CFA, CIC

President/CEO
Senior Portfolio Manager
James Investment Research, Inc.

Chairman/President
James Advantage Funds,
a mutual fund family

Chairman/CEO
James Capital Alliance

Barry James was James Investment Research, Inc.'s first paid employee before attending the U.S. Air Force Academy. After graduating, he served an eight-year tour as a USAF instructor and fighter pilot. He returned to JIR in 1986.

He was awarded a master's degree in business administration with a letter of honors from Boston University in 1987. He holds the designations of Chartered Financial Analyst and Chartered Investment Counsel, which together recognize significant expertise, analytical skill and ethical standards in the field of investment management.

Barry serves as chairman of the James Capital Alliance and James Advantage Funds boards, as board secretary for the Heart to Honduras mission, and on the board of directors for the Dayton Area Chamber of Commerce. He was named the Dayton Business Journal's Business Leader of the Year in 2007.

He currently oversees the management of James Investment Research and is a senior member of its Investment Committee, conducting extensive research on both the stock and bond markets.

Barry is a recognized authority on investments, often quoted by major financial news organizations, and is a frequent guest commentator on television and radio programs.

To learn more about Barry and his thoughts on God-Honoring Business Principles, visit his personal website at barryrjames.com.

To contact Barry for speaking engagements or investment information, call 937-426-7640 or email jir@jir-inc.com.

About James Investment Research, Inc.

James Investment Research, Inc. was founded in 1972 to help clients achieve their long-term financial goals while following the highest standards of ethics and timeless investment principles. In 2011, the firm exceeded $3.0 billion in assets under management.

The firm works with new and experienced investors with assets ranging from $50 to $50 million. It provides life-long financial management through its mutual funds, separately managed accounts, and private portfolio management.

JIR's motto is *"Investing For A Lifetime."*

VISION

To be recognized as the best investment firm in America. Through striving to follow God-honoring principles, its goal is to spearhead a dramatic improvement in the reputation of the financial investing industry.

The investing public will finally have peace of mind because all firms will put their clients' interests first and achieve those clients' financial goals.

MISSION

The JIR team of professionals is committed to providing clients with peace of mind through time-proven research, premier service and consistently superior investment performance.

The company is dedicated to supporting and respecting its team, clients and community, an approach JIR believes will provide the rewards of continued growth and shared profitability.

HONORS

- Past recognition by Lipper, *The Wall Street Journal* and *Morningstar*.

- Three-time Community Supporter of the Year, *Dayton Business Journal*

- Frequent mentions in *Barron's*, *The Wall Street Journal, Smart Money*, and other major financial publications

MORE INFORMATION

James Investment Research, Inc.

P.O. Box 8, Alpha OH 45301

1.888.426.7640

JIR-INC.COM